Dedicated to my parents
and my sister Elsa, the first to graduate
and lead the way.

www.LilLibros.com

Sábado / Saturday
Published in the United States by Lil' Libros

Copyright © 2022 Jorge Garza

Library of Congress Control Number 2021945315

Printed in China

First Edition, 2022
27 26 25 24 23 22   5 4 3 2 1

ISBN 978-1-948066-10-5

Sábado

Saturday

Jorge Garza

Lil' LIBROS

Domingo
Sunday

Taller de Costura
Yolanda
Sewing Workshop

Lunes
Monday

Martes
Tuesday

COLOR FLOWERS

XOCHITL
Flores • Flowers

Miércoles
Wednesday

Jueves
Thursday

Viernes
Friday

Sábado
Saturday

If you have this book in your hands, *tlazocamati* (thank you)!
Aztec (Mexica) art, specifically the codices, is the inspiration for the drawings in *Sábado*. My goal is to honor the past and present as well as bring attention to the beautiful Meso-American cultures and art. I hope this book inspires children, especially brown and indigenous, to draw, learn about their culture, and be proud of who they are and where they come from.

Jorge Garza is a Mexican-American illustrator from Indiana, where he currently resides. Jorge is best known for an art style mashing up Aztec art and pop culture called Azteca Pop. Jorge's art went viral with his Azteca Pop drawings of various cultural icons and his ongoing art series highlighting essential and frontline workers. His artwork has exhibited at the National Museum of Mexican Art in Chicago as well as the Amor Eterno art gallery in Oakland. He also enjoys writing and drawing his own comic books.